HYPNOSIS 101

A Beginner's Guide To Unlocking The Power Of The Mind

Bill Gonzales

Ukiyoto Publishing

All global publishing rights are held by

Ukiyoto Publishing

Published in 2023

Content Copyright © Bill Gonzales

ISBN 9789359203898

All rights reserved.
No part of this publication may be reproduced, transmitted, or stored in a retrieval system, in any form by any means, electronic, mechanical, photocopying, recording or otherwise, without the prior permission of the publisher.

The moral rights of the author have been asserted.

This book is sold subject to the condition that it shall not by way of trade or otherwise, be lent, resold, hired out or otherwise circulated, without the publisher's prior consent, in any form of binding or cover other than that in which it is published.

www.ukiyoto.com

Dedication

First of all, I would like to thank God, who gave me the wisdom, knowledge and understanding that allows me to master this craft to help a lot of people, to my parents Tony and Gina Gonzales, to my partner Jen Chua who keeps inspiring me and pushing me forward to achieve my dreams and goals, to my mentors and coaches in NLP and Hypnosis who guides me continuously, sharing their knowledge, skills and wisdom for personal growth and development, my colleagues in the NLP and Hypnosis world, and to my friends who supports me all the way.

I also dedicate this to all aspiring hypnotist who intends to help people in need. May this book help you understand how to do hypnosis and may you be able to use this as a tool to change someone's world.

Contents

Introduction	1
Demystifying Hypnosis - Myths and Facts	4
Mastering the Basics of Hypnosis	8
Deepeners and Suggestions – Going Deeper Into The	23
Subconscious Mind	23
Self-Hypnosis	28
Bringing the Subject Out of Trance	33
Identifying Trance Signs	36
The Art of Observation	37
Physical Indicators of Trance Signs	40
Verbal Trance Indicators	43
Understanding Abreactions in Hypnosis	47
The Power of Hypnotic Language: The Power Words	50
Building Instant Rapport	54
Mastering Compliance for Effective Inductions	57
Exploring Hypnosis Careers and Embracing the Art To Help Other People	62
About the Author	*69*

Introduction

Welcome to the world of hypnosis! Where the mind's untapped potential awaits your exploration. As a Consulting Hypnotist, Hypnotherapist, and NLP practitioner, I am thrilled to take you on this extraordinary journey of self-discovery and empowerment by understanding the basics of hypnosis. If you've ever been curious about the power of the mind and how it can be harnessed to create positive change, then you have the right book! .

Before we dive into the depths of hypnosis, let me share a little about myself and why I am so passionate about this what you call "hypnosis". My name is Bill Gonzales, and throughout my career as a nurse turned entrepreneur, I have had the privilege of witnessing the incredible transformation that hypnosis can bring to people's lives. I have seen clients and students experience profound growth and success through the internal changes simply by understanding the subconscious mind and how suggestions works.

Perhaps you are already familiar with my previous book, "Mind Mastery: 21-Day Journey to Mastering Manifestation, Personal Growth, and Success." If not, in that book, we delved into the art of manifestation and the power of the mind in shaping our reality. Through my work with hypnosis and NLP, I discovered that these techniques are potent tools for achieving one's goals and overcoming obstacles.

The essence of hypnosis lies in understanding the power of suggestion, power of words and understanding the subconscious mind. We all have a deep untapped potential residing within us, waiting to be accessed and harnessed for our benefit. Hypnosis allows us to tap into this untapped potential and make lasting changes by influencing the subconscious mind positively.

Imagine if you could be able to let go of limiting beliefs, conquer fears, and develop unshakable confidence. Hypnosis offers you the key to unlock the doors to your mind's potential and empower yourself to create the life you desire.

In this book, "Hypnosis 101: A Beginner's Guide to Unlocking the Power of the Mind," I aim to provide you with a step-by-step guide to mastering the art of hypnosis. Whether you're a complete beginner or someone seeking to enhance their existing knowledge, this book will equip you with the necessary tools to perform hypnotic inductions effectively.

Throughout the pages of this book, you will learn how to prepare your mind for hypnosis, utilize relaxation techniques, and understand the art of inducing hypnosis in others. We will explore various hypnotic induction methods, such as the Arm Drop Technique, Arm Pull Method, Eye Fixation Technique, and Progressive Muscle Relaxation.

Moreover, I will introduce you to the incredible realm of self-hypnosis, where you can take charge of your personal growth and positive change. Self-hypnosis is a powerful skill that empowers you to overcome challenges, reduce stress, and cultivate a mindset for success.

As you immerse yourself in the world of hypnosis, you will discover the applications and techniques used to address various issues such as stress management, overcoming fears and phobias, and even pain management.

The ability to influence the subconscious mind through hypnosis can be a life-changing skill. In this book, we will explore how you can use hypnosis to make a positive impact on people's lives, including your own. Additionally, I will guide you on the path to becoming a Hypnotist, should you choose to pursue a career in this field.

Now, I invite you to embark on this transformative journey of self-discovery and empowerment through the power of suggestions. Embrace the power of suggestion and the immense potential of your subconscious mind. By the end of this book, you will possess the knowledge and skills to confidently practice hypnosis, create positive change, and unlock the door to endless possibilities.

Remember, the power to succeed and achieve greatness lies within you. Let's take this incredible voyage together as we delve into the world of "Hypnosis" and learn to unleash the power of the mind!

Demystifying Hypnosis - Myths and Facts

Hypnosis is a natural state of heightened awareness and focused concentration, often described as a trance-like state. In this state, individuals experience a heightened sense of relaxation and are more open to suggestions. Contrary to popular belief, hypnosis is not a state of unconsciousness or sleep (how can you give a suggestion to an unconscious person?); rather, it is a state of deep relaxation where the conscious mind takes a step back, allowing the subconscious mind to take the forefront.

Hypnosis has long been surrounded by misconceptions, often perpetuated by the media and stage performances. It is time to set the record straight and address some of the **common myths associated with hypnosis.**

1. Mind Control: One of the most prevalent misconceptions is that hypnosis involves mind control, where the hypnotist can manipulate the subject's thoughts and actions. In reality, hypnosis is a state of heightened focus and suggestibility, where the subject retains full control over their thoughts and actions. If it is against their value, the subject has full control to get out of trance.

2. Loss of Consciousness: Another myth is that hypnotized individuals are in a state of unconsciousness or sleep. On the contrary, hypnosis induces a deep state of relaxation and heightened awareness, akin to daydreaming or meditation. Imagine talking to an unconscious person? It's like talking to a dummy! Hehe!

3. Vulnerability to Manipulation: It is often believed that people under hypnosis can be made to do anything against their will. In truth, individuals in a hypnotic state will only respond to suggestions that align with their core beliefs and values.

4. Memory Retrieval: Hypnosis is not a foolproof method for retrieving accurate memories. While it can enhance recall in some cases, memories can be influenced and altered, leading to false recollections.

Hypnosis is more than just a parlor trick; it is a scientifically validated and well-researched field with a rich history of study and practice.

1. Brain Activity: Neuroimaging studies have revealed that hypnosis alters brain activity, leading to changes in perception, memory, and consciousness. Specific brain regions are activated during hypnosis, highlighting its neurobiological basis.

2. Therapeutic Applications: Hypnosis has gained recognition in the medical and therapeutic communities for its effectiveness in pain management, stress reduction, and treatment of various psychological conditions.

3. Altered State of Consciousness: Hypnosis induces a trance-like state, characterized by heightened suggestibility and focused attention. During this state, individuals experience a shift in consciousness, allowing them to explore their subconscious mind.

4. Placebo and Nocebo Effects: Hypnosis shares similarities with the placebo effect, where positive beliefs lead to positive outcomes. Conversely, the nocebo effect can occur when negative expectations produce adverse effects.

The subconscious mind plays a pivotal role in the process of hypnosis. It is the part of the mind responsible for storing memories, emotions, beliefs, and habits. Hypnosis allows access to this deeper level of the mind, enabling positive changes through the power of suggestion.

Hypnosis and the Power of Suggestion

The power of suggestion is at the core of hypnosis. During a hypnotic session, the hypnotist provides positive and constructive suggestions that can influence the subject's thoughts and behaviors. These suggestions, when aligned with the individual's goals and values, can create profound transformations.

The term "hypnotic trance" refers to the state of focused concentration and heightened suggestibility induced during hypnosis. It is not a state of unconsciousness but rather a deep state of relaxation where the conscious mind takes a backseat, allowing the subconscious mind to take the forefront.

In the next chapters, we will explore various hypnotic induction techniques, relaxation methods, and the art of crafting effective suggestions. By understanding the science behind hypnosis and debunking common myths, you will be better equipped to embrace the power of hypnosis and utilize it to enhance your life. It is evident that hypnosis is a legitimate and powerful tool for personal growth and transformation. By dispelling the myths and understanding the scientific basis of hypnosis, we can harness its potential to achieve positive change in our lives. In the following chapters, we will continue this journey of discovery and dive deeper into the practical applications of hypnosis, including the art of hypnotic inductions and the empowerment of the subconscious mind. So, get ready to embark on an exciting adventure into the world of hypnosis and unlock the hidden abilities of your mind!

Mastering the Basics of Hypnosis

This chapter is your gateway to mastering the art of hypnosis and becoming a skilled hypnotist. Whether you're looking to perform street or stage hypnosis or simply want to harness the power of hypnosis for personal growth and transformation, this chapter will equip you with essential techniques and insights.

Before we proceed with hypnosis, let's break down the mind's layers in a technical yet simple way using the iceberg analogy so that you can easily understand what part of the mind we are working with during hypnosis:

Comparing the mind to an iceberg helps us understand its complexity. Just like an iceberg has hidden depths, the mind has layers:

1. **Conscious Mind: The Active Thinker**

Imagine the conscious mind as the part of the iceberg above the water – it's what you're aware of most of the time. It's like the control room where you think, solve problems, and make decisions. When you're reading, chatting, or solving puzzles, your conscious mind is on the job.

2. **Critical Mind: The Protective Filter**

Think of the critical mind as the iceberg's surface, protecting what's underneath. It's like a gatekeeper, checking if new info matches what you already know. It's the reason you might doubt new ideas – it wants to keep things consistent. Just like waves hitting the iceberg's surface, new info hits your critical mind for evaluation.

3. Subconscious Mind: The Memory Vault

Underneath the water's surface is the subconscious mind, much like the submerged part of an iceberg. It's where your memories, habits, and feelings hang out. When you do things without thinking, like riding a bike, that's your subconscious mind at play. It's like an archive of all your experiences.

4. Unconscious Mind: The Automatic Pilot

Deeper down, we have the unconscious mind – kind of like the iceberg's hidden base. This is where automatic stuff happens, like breathing and reflexes. It's also where deep emotions and instincts reside. Like the iceberg's foundational support, the unconscious mind keeps your body functioning smoothly.

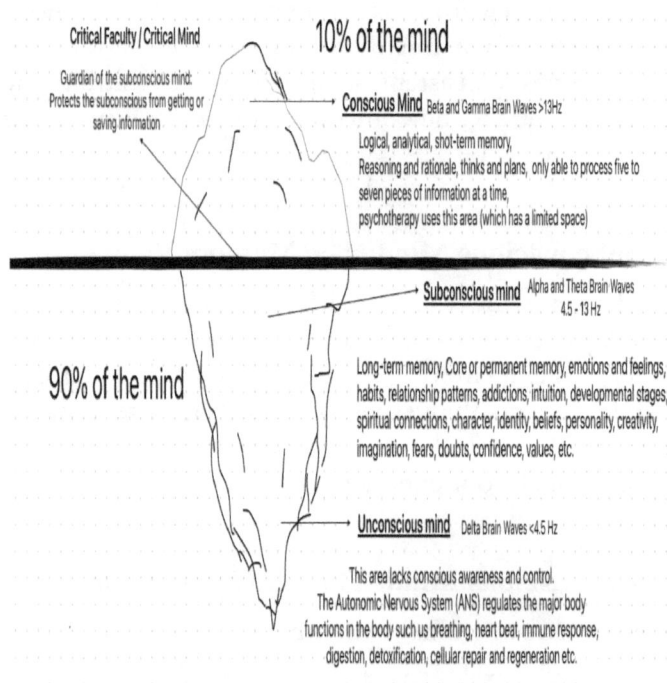

Understanding these layers helps us see how our mind works together, just like an iceberg's parts. By knowing how the conscious, critical faculty, subconscious, and unconscious minds interact, we can navigate our thoughts, behaviors, and emotions more effectively. It's like having a map to explore the fascinating world within our minds.

Now that you are familiar with the levels of the mind, we can now proceed to hypnosis!

The Hypnosis Formula

Alright, let's talk about hypnosis in a way that anyone can get. We've got this cool formula called **ABS – Attention, Bypass, Suggest**. It's like the magic recipe for getting your mind into a super focused and open state. Hypnosis will only revolve in this formula. Once you understand applying this ABS formula, it will be very easy for you to do hypnosis and self hypnosis.

A - Attention: Get Hooked

First thing's first, we need to grab someone's full attention. Imagine seeing your crush around or he or she is within the area, what happens? Imagine watching a climax of a movie that you really love, you are so focused that your peripheral attention starts to shrink. Hypnotists use interesting stories, patterns, or even just super engaging words to make you go, "Hey, what's this all about?" It's like getting you to stop and listen up.

B - Bypass the conscious mind: Sneak In

Now that we've got your attention, we gotta sneak past that little voice in your head that's always questioning things. You know, that "wait a minute, is this for real?" voice. We call that voice your "**Critical Faculty**" the guardian of your subconscious mind. The Critical faculty, others calls it critical mind protects your subconscious because your subconscious mind is where your beliefs, character, personality, long term memory, and identity is stored. Now to bypass the critical faculty, We do that by confusing it a bit, overloading it, getting it shocked or helping it relax so the mind will stop overthinking. It's like getting into a secret club without showing your ID – you're in, and that voice is taking a break.

S - Suggest: Planting Ideas

Here's where the real fun happens. We start talking to your mind in a way that makes it go, "Hmm, I never thought of that before." We're like planting awesome ideas in your brain garden. These ideas are all about helping you reach your goals – whether it's feeling more confident or kicking a bad habit. We use words that make those ideas stick, like a catchy song you can't stop humming.

Here's the simple summary of the formula:

So, there you have it, the ABS formula. It's like catching your attention, sneaking past the doubting voice, and planting cool ideas in your mind garden. It's a neat way to help you be your best self and achieve things you want. So by understanding this simple hypnosis formula, you can understand how the techniques that I wrote in this book works.

Hypnotic Inductions

What is Hypnotic Induction?

"Hypnotic induction is a process done by a hypnotist to lead the subject into trance or

a series of instructions or actions done by a hypnotist to help someone achieve trance state."

Before we dive into the induction techniques, let's explore some essential tips to effectively hypnotize someone:

1. **Building rapport** is the foundation of a successful hypnosis session. Establish a genuine connection with your subject through active listening and empathy. Make them feel comfortable and safe, fostering trust and cooperation.

2. **Suggestibility Tests and Compliance Tests:** Before inducing hypnosis, it's crucial to gauge the subject's suggestibility. Suggestibility tests help you assess how receptive the individual is to hypnosis. A popular suggestibility test is the Hand Levitation Test. Instruct the subject to extend their arms, palms facing each other, and imagine balloons tied to their wrists. Suggest that the balloons are lifting their hands upward. Those whose hands rise are more likely to be receptive to hypnosis. Compliance tests are designed to determine the subject's willingness to follow suggestions. These tests serve as precursors to the induction process, ensuring that the subject is open to the hypnotic experience. Here are two simple and effective suggestibility with compliance tests:

a) **Hand Clasp Test**:

Ask the subject to clasp their hands together firmly, then ask them to close their eyes. Then, suggest that they imagine their hands are stuck together, becoming tightly locked. Now, instruct them to try and pull their hands apart while maintaining that they will find it challenging to do so.

Sample Script:

"Now, I want you to clasp your hands together, interlocking your fingers. Now, close your eyes and Imagine that your hands are starting to feel stuck, magnetically drawn to each other, becoming tightly locked. Now, try to pull your hands apart and notice how they become stuck together, as if they were one solid piece."

b) **Eye Closure Test:**

Guide the subject to gently close their eyes and then suggest that their eyes are becoming so heavy and relaxed that it would be challenging to open them.

Sample Script:

"As you allow your eyes to close, you'll notice a deep sense of relaxation washing over you. Your eyelids are becoming so comfortably heavy that you won't even want to try to open them."

By observing the subject's response to these compliance tests, you can gain valuable insights into their level of suggestibility and readiness for hypnosis. Subjects who readily comply are more likely to be cooperative during the induction process.

Now, let's explore three powerful hypnotic induction techniques, complete with step-by-step instructions and sample scripts:

Eye Fixation Induction:

Step 1: Set the Scene and Relaxation

Start by guiding the subject into a state of relaxation:

"Take a deep breath in, and as you exhale, allow any tension in your body to melt away. Feel yourself becoming more and more relaxed with each breath you take."

Step 2: Establish Eye Contact and Focus

Instruct the subject to focus their gaze on a specific object or point:

"Keep your eyes on this point and feel yourself becoming more focused and centered. Your eyes are getting heavier and heavier as you continue to concentrate on this spot."

Step 3: Utilize a Calm and Soothing Voice

Use a soothing voice to deepen their relaxation:

"Allow yourself to relax completely now. You are safe and supported. Let my voice guide you into a deeper state of tranquility."

Step 4: Suggest Relaxation and Deepening

Use positive affirmations and suggestions to deepen relaxation:

"Feel the warmth of relaxation spreading through your body, from the top of your head to the tips of your toes. With each breath you take, you become more deeply relaxed.

You can use 5-1 deepener:

"Now, as I count from 5 to 1, you will start to feel more deeply, and more relaxed.

5…4…3…2…1… all the way down deeper and more relaxed"

Arm Drop Induction:

Step 1: Create a Safe and Trusting Atmosphere

Build trust and reassurance:

"Know that you are always in control during this process. At any time, you can open your eyes and become fully awake if you choose."

Step 2: Have the Subject Hold Out Their Arm

Instruct the subject to hold their arm out parallel to the floor:

"I want you to hold your arm out like this, and as you do, imagine a stream of relaxation flowing from your shoulder, all the way down to your fingertips."

Step 3: Use Suggestion to Induce Relaxation

Suggest that the arm is becoming heavier and more relaxed:

"As you continue to focus on your arm, you may notice it becoming pleasantly heavy and relaxed. This is a sign that you are allowing yourself to enter into a comfortable and peaceful state."

Step 4: Sudden Hand Drop and Deepening Techniques

With a sudden hand drop or gentle push on the subject's arm, induce complete relaxation:

"Now, I'm going to gently drop your hand. As it drops, you will go even deeper into relaxation. Trust yourself and allow this feeling of calmness to embrace you fully."

Body Scan Induction:

Step 1: Prepare the Subject for Relaxation

Guide the subject to a comfortable position and have them focus on their breath:

"Find a comfortable position, and with each breath you take, let go of any tension or stress you may be holding onto."

Step 2: Guide the Subject's Attention to Their Body

Use visualization to lead the subject's attention through their body:

"Imagine a warm, soothing light shining down on the top of your head, bringing with it a sense of relaxation and ease. Allow this light to gently wash over you, moving down your body, relaxing every muscle and every fiber."

Step 3: Suggest Progressive Relaxation

Suggest increasing levels of relaxation in each body part:

"Feel this wave of relaxation moving down your face, your neck, and your shoulders. As it continues down to your chest and arms, notice how every muscle becomes loose and limp, loose and limp, loose and limp, like a soft, relaxed rubber band."

Step 4: Deepening and Focusing the Mind

Use affirmations to deepen the trance and enhance focus:

"Allow yourself to drift deeper and deeper into this state of profound relaxation. Your mind is clear and focused, ready to embrace positive changes and transformation."

Now for my personal favorite induction, a shock induction…

Armpull Induction:

Step 1: Prepare the Subject

Ensure that the subject is comfortably seated or standing, with both feet planted firmly on the ground. Create a relaxed atmosphere and reassure the subject that they are safe and in control at all times.

Step 2: Gain Consent

Always obtain verbal consent from the subject before proceeding with any induction technique.

Step 3: Establish Eye Contact and Rapport

Maintain eye contact with the subject and establish rapport through friendly and positive communication. This will foster trust and cooperation during the induction process.

Step 4: Instruct the Subject to Extend Their Arm

Ask the subject to extend one of their arms in front of them, hold their wrist and lightly shake their arm until you feel that the arm is totally relaxed. Instruct them to keep the arm relaxed and limp, as if it were a loose rubber band.

Step 5: Use Suggestion to Induce Relaxation

Use a calm and soothing tone to guide the subject into a state of relaxation:

"As you keep your arm extended, imagine a sense of relaxation flowing from your shoulder, all the way down to your fingertips. Feel your arm becoming heavier and more relaxed with each breath you take."

Step 6: Demonstrate the Arm Pull

Now, demonstrate the arm pull induction. Surprisingly pull the subject's arm with one hand gently (don't pull so hard, pull their arm quickly but gentle enough to make them out of balance to create a shock) then say "SLEEP! All the way down deeper and more relaxed" simultaneously when you pull the arm.

(Important Note: Some hypnotic subjects are highly suggestive and will literally become like a ragdoll. Make sure to catch them or suggest to maintakn their balance after pulling their arm and saying sleep.)

Step 7: Encourage the Subject to Relax

Encourage the subject to continue relaxing their whole body and maintaining their balance and allow you to guide them.

"Allow your whole body to feel loose and heavy, just like a ragdoll. Trust that I will gently guide you, and all you need to do is let go and allow yourself to relax even deeper.".

Remember to proceed with care and sensitivity during the induction process, ensuring that the subject feels comfortable and safe throughout the experience. The armpull induction is a powerful technique to induce hypnosis quickly and effectively, allowing you to explore the fascinating world of the subconscious mind.

Congratulations! You've now learned some hypnotic induction techniques, along with compliance tests to ensure successful hypnosis sessions. Make sure to keep on practicing since this is a skill that needs actual experience. Don't feel bad if it doesn't work at first, what's important is for you to practice!

(PRO TIP: If you want to be a great street/stage hypnotist or hypnotic performer, the best tip that I can give you is to master identifying the perfect subject, the highly suggestive people by mastering the suggestibility tests.)

Deepeners and Suggestions – Going Deeper Into The Subconscious Mind

In the previous chapters, we have learned the basics of hypnosis and how to induce a hypnotic state. Now, it's time to take our exploration to a deeper level. In this chapter, we will explore the art of deepening the hypnotic state and delivering powerful suggestions to effect positive change in the subconscious mind.

The Importance of Deepeners

A deepener is an essential component of hypnosis that takes the subject from a light trance to a more profound state of relaxation and receptivity. Deepeners allow us to bypass the critical faculty (guardian of the subconscious), making the subconscious mind more open to suggestions. Remember that every individual's experience is unique, so be attentive to the subject's responses and adjust the deepener as needed.

Script: Progressive Relaxation Deepener

"Now, take a deep breath and as you exhale, imagine a golden light at your toes. This light is warm and soothing, spreading relaxation to every muscle it touches. Feel it traveling slowly up your body, melting away any tension it encounters. With each breath, the golden light moves upward, leaving a trail of tranquility in its wake. You feel a sense of profound calmness and peace as it reaches your head. You are completely relaxed, your mind open and receptive to positive suggestions."

Script: Visualization Deepener

"Close your eyes and take a moment to imagine yourself floating on a soft, fluffy cloud. Feel the gentle support of the cloud beneath you, as it carries you effortlessly across the clear blue sky. As you float, you notice all your worries and stress begin to fade away, replaced by a sense of serenity and joy. With each breath, you feel lighter and more carefree, embracing the freedom of this tranquil journey. You are safe and at ease, ready to explore the depths of your subconscious mind."

Script: Imagery Deepener

"Imagine yourself strolling through a beautiful, blossoming garden. The air is filled with the fragrance of vibrant flowers, and the sun warms your skin with a gentle caress. As you walk, you feel the softness of the grass beneath your feet, connecting you to the earth's soothing energy. The garden is a sanctuary of peace and tranquility, and you feel completely at ease and at one with nature. This serene environment opens the doorway to your subconscious mind, where positive change awaits."

Tailored Suggestions for Personal Transformation

As hypnotists, we have the incredible opportunity to assist individuals in achieving their goals and overcoming challenges. Delivering tailored suggestions based on their specific needs is the key to unlocking the full potential of hypnosis. Whether it's boosting self-confidence, overcoming fears, or enhancing performance, the right suggestions can create remarkable transformations.

Script: Creating Tailored Suggestions for Specific Goals

[Scenario: For weight loss]

"Imagine yourself standing in front of a mirror, seeing the reflection of your ideal self looking back at you. You feel a deep sense of love and acceptance for your body, appreciating all the incredible things it does for you. Now, visualize yourself making healthy choices each day, nourishing your body with wholesome foods that fuel your energy and vitality. See yourself engaging in regular physical activity with enthusiasm, knowing that each step brings you closer to your ideal weight. You are in complete control of your eating habits, and you find joy in making positive choices for your health.

Your body is a temple of strength and wellness, and you radiate confidence and self-assurance in every aspect of your life."

Compliance Tests - Building Trust and Rapport

Before delivering suggestions, it is crucial to build rapport and establish trust with the subject. Compliance tests are a valuable tool in accomplishing this. By incorporating simple, non-invasive tests, we gauge the subject's responsiveness and willingness to follow instructions. These tests also serve as effective deepeners, as they engage the subject's imagination and reinforce their susceptibility to hypnosis.

Scenario: Hand Levitation Compliance Test

"Let's try a simple compliance test to see how relaxed you are. Extend your arm in front of you and imagine it becoming lighter, as if it's attached to a bunch of helium balloons. Now, see if you can allow that arm to gently rise, floating effortlessly toward the ceiling. You may notice a sensation of lightness as it rises. Don't force it; just allow it to happen naturally. This test helps us gauge your responsiveness to suggestion and provides valuable feedback on your level of trance."

In this chapter, we've delved into the powerful art of deepening the hypnotic state and delivering customized suggestions. Remember that mastering the skill of hypnosis is an ongoing journey, and each individual's experience is unique. With practice and dedication, you'll become more adept at guiding others on a transformative voyage within their subconscious minds.

Self-Hypnosis

In the previous chapters, we've explored the wonders of hypnosis and its applications in various aspects of life. Now, it's time to dive into the world of self-hypnosis—a practice that empowers you to unlock the potential of your subconscious mind and take charge of your personal growth journey.

Self-hypnosis is the process of inducing a hypnotic state in oneself, allowing for heightened focus and suggestibility. Unlike traditional hypnosis, where a hypnotist guides the process, self-hypnosis puts you in control, making it a powerful tool for personal transformation. You don't need any special skills to begin; it's a natural state that we all experience daily, like being engrossed in a book or daydreaming.

Central to self-hypnosis is the understanding of suggestion and its impact on the subconscious mind. By consciously directing your thoughts and beliefs, you can tap into the immense power of your subconscious, rewiring negative thought patterns, and instilling positive affirmations for personal growth and success.

Introducing BillyG's 3-2-1 Method:

As a practitioner of hypnosis and personal development, I'm thrilled to share with you my own self-hypnosis technique—the BillyG's 3-2-1 Method. This powerful method combines mindfulness and relaxation to help you access the depths of your subconscious mind.

Step 1: Three Objects

Find a comfortable and quiet space to practice the 3-2-1 Method. Take a few deep breaths to center yourself. Now, identify three objects within your surroundings—one at a time. Gently shift your focus from one object to the next, observing their details, colors, and shapes. As you concentrate on each object, allow yourself to slowly take deep breaths and feel your body relaxing with each breath. Embrace the present moment fully, immersing yourself in the experience of observing these objects.

Step 2: Two Sounds

Next, bring your attention to your sense of hearing. Identify two sounds around you—a distant bird chirping, the hum of a fan, or any other sounds in your environment. As you listen to these sounds, let them become the focal point of your awareness. With each sound, take deep breaths and feel any tension in your body melt away. Allow yourself to fully engage with the auditory experience, letting go of any distracting thoughts.

Step 3: One Sensation

Now, shift your focus to your sense of touch. Identify one sensation you feel in your body—a gentle breeze against your skin, the texture of a surface you're touching, or the comfort of your clothing. Direct your attention solely to this sensation, exploring its nuances and subtleties. As you embrace this sensation, take deep breaths and let any stress or worries dissipate. Allow yourself to become fully attuned to this sensation and the relaxation it brings.

By the end of the 3-2-1 Method, you will have engaged all your senses, heightening your mindfulness and inner focus. This state of heightened awareness and relaxation allows you to access the power of your subconscious mind and makes you more receptive to positive suggestions and affirmations.

Other Self-Hypnosis Techniques:

Beyond the 3-2-1 Method, there are various self-hypnosis techniques you can explore to enhance your well-being and personal growth. Here are some popular ones:

1. Visualization: Create vivid mental images of your desired outcomes and experiences. By visualizing success and positivity, you're planting seeds of transformation in your subconscious mind.

2. Affirmations: Craft positive statements that reflect your goals and intentions. Repeat these affirmations

regularly during self-hypnosis sessions to reinforce your belief in your capabilities.

3. Guided Imagery: Use recorded or written scripts to guide yourself through relaxing and transformative visualizations. These scripts can focus on specific goals like overcoming fears or boosting self-confidence.

4. Breathing Techniques: Incorporate different breathing patterns into your self-hypnosis practice. Deep, rhythmic breathing helps induce relaxation and calms the mind.

5. Progressive Muscle Relaxation: Systematically tense and then release each muscle group in your body. This technique helps release physical tension and promotes overall relaxation.

6. Inner Dialogue: Engage in positive self-talk during your self-hypnosis sessions. Replace self-doubt with self-assurance and encourage yourself to believe in your potential.

Remember, self-hypnosis is a personal journey of self-discovery, and the techniques that resonate with you may differ from others. Explore these methods and find the ones that align with your goals and preferences. These powerful techniques can take your self-hypnosis practice to new depths, leading to profound personal transformations. So, continue to embrace the wonders of self-hypnosis, and open yourself to the endless possibilities of your mind. You are the conductor of your subconscious symphony, and through self-hypnosis, you have the power to create harmonious and positive changes in your life.

Bringing the Subject Out of Trance

Bringing a subject out of hypnosis is as important as inducing a trance. A smooth and gentle awakening process ensures a positive and safe experience for the subject. Here's a step-by-step guide to effectively guide your subject back to full awareness:

1. Gradual Awakening:

To ensure a smooth transition, gently guide the subject back to the waking state. Use a calm and soothing tone, informing them that they will awaken gradually, feeling refreshed and energized. Count slowly from one to five, assuring them that with each count, they will return to full awareness.

2. Post-Hypnotic Suggestions:

Prior to awakening, incorporate post-hypnotic suggestions into the subject's subconscious mind. These suggestions can serve as reinforcement for the positive changes and transformations experienced during the session. For instance, you can suggest increased confidence, improved focus, or a sense of inner peace.

Sample Script:

"As I count from 1 to 5, slowly get out of trance, feeling good, feeling great, refreshed and energized! 1... 2... 3... get out of trance... 4... 5! (Snap your fingers) Wide Awake!"

3. Follow-Up Support:

After the session, offer support and guidance to your subjects. Provide them with resources or techniques they can use independently to reinforce the benefits of hypnosis. This can include self-hypnosis scripts, affirmations, or mindfulness exercises to maintain the progress achieved during the session.

4. Safety Considerations:

As a responsible hypnotist, prioritize the safety and well-being of your subjects. During the awakening process, ensure that the subject is fully alert and oriented before allowing them to resume regular activities. Avoid abrupt awakenings, as they can lead to disorientation or dizziness.

5. Addressing Emotional Responses:

Some subjects may experience emotional responses during or after the session. Approach any emotional expressions with empathy and understanding. Allow them to express their feelings and provide a safe space for processing their experiences.

6. Debriefing Session:

Consider conducting a debriefing session with your subjects after they have fully awakened. This provides an opportunity for open communication, allowing them to share their experiences and ask any questions they may have. Address any concerns and offer additional guidance or clarification as needed.

Remember, each individual responds differently to hypnosis, so be flexible in your approach. Some subjects may awaken feeling energized and uplifted, while others may require a few moments to reorient themselves. By practicing patience and compassion, you can create a positive hypnosis experience for your subjects, promoting long-lasting positive changes and personal growth.

Identifying Trance Signs

The Art of Observation

In hypnosis, the skill of keen observation plays a vital role, setting exceptional hypnotists apart from the rest. The ability to detect and interpret subtle signs and cues that indicate a subject's entry into a trance state is fundamental in conducting successful hypnosis sessions. As a hypnotist, your proficiency in observation empowers you to fine-tune your approach and tailor suggestions to the unique needs of each individual.

Effective observation commences with focused attention. As you guide your subject into hypnosis, keep your senses attuned to their responses, paying close attention to their body language, facial expressions, and vocal cues. Observe any shifts in their demeanor, such as a change in posture, muscle relaxation, or a softened gaze, all indicative of a change in mental state.

Nonverbal cues hold remarkable significance during the induction process. Look for signs of relaxation, like slow and steady breathing, a slackening of muscles, and a softened gaze. These physical manifestations often signify the subject's entry into a state of heightened receptivity, suggesting that they are gradually slipping into a hypnotic trance.

During the induction, be attentive to subtle changes in speech. Listen for variations in tone, pace, and choice of words, as these may reflect the subject's altered state of consciousness. Their speech may take on a soothing rhythm, more deliberate articulation, or a preference for imaginative language. These shifts offer valuable insights into their level of suggestibility.

Observing eye movement can serve as a window into the subject's mind during hypnosis. As they enter a trance, their eyes may flutter or fixate on a focal point (similar to day dreaming), indicating an increased absorption of your suggestions. This eye behavior can be instrumental in gauging their level of immersion in the hypnotic experience.

Your intuition as a hypnotist will naturally develop and refine over time. Trust your instincts as you interact with your subjects, allowing your intuition to guide you in adjusting your techniques and pacing to align with their unique responsiveness. In parallel, engaging in mindfulness practices outside of hypnosis can significantly enhance your observation skills. Cultivate a mindful mindset in your daily life, honing your ability to be fully present and aware. This mindfulness will naturally extend to your hypnosis sessions, enabling you to be more perceptive and empathetic toward your subjects' experiences.

Mastering the art of observation opens doors to creating profound and transformative experiences for your subjects. The deeper your understanding of their responses, the more adept you'll become at crafting personalized and impactful suggestions. As you embark on your journey in learning hypnosis , remember that the art of observation is an ongoing practice, continuously evolving and refining with each new session.

Physical Indicators of Trance Signs

1. Slow and Steady Breathing: The subject's breath becomes calmer and more rhythmic, reflecting a state of deep relaxation.

2. Muscle Relaxation: A gradual release of muscle tension, leading to a limp or slackened posture.

3. Eye Fixation: The subject's gaze may become fixated on a specific point, exhibiting reduced eye movement.

4. Fluttering Eyelids: Occasional fluttering or slight twitching of the eyelids during relaxation.

5. Dilated Pupils: Pupils may appear larger and more responsive to light.

6. Swallowing: Decreased frequency of swallowing as relaxation deepens.

7. Microexpressions: Subtle, fleeting facial expressions, such as a slight smile or raised eyebrows.

8. Numbness or Tingling Sensations: Some subjects may experience a sensation of numbness or tingling in various body parts.

9. Limb Heaviness: The limbs may feel heavy or anchored to the surface they are resting on.

10. Catalepsy: A condition in which the subject's limbs remain in a fixed position when placed by the hypnotist.

11. Lacrimation: Tear secretion, indicating emotional release during hypnosis.

12. Skin Color Changes: The skin may appear paler due to decreased blood flow.

13. Sighing: Occasional deep sighs as the subject releases tension.

14. Speech Changes: Speech may slow down or become more deliberate and rhythmic.

15. Hand Levitation: The subject's hand may involuntarily rise when prompted by the hypnotist.

16. Increased Salivation: A noticeable increase in saliva production during relaxation.

17. Eye Closure: The eyes may remain closed or droop as the subject enters a deeper trance.

18. Blank Facial Expression: A serene and vacant facial expression, devoid of tension.

19. Rapid Eye Movement: Despite overall relaxation, subjects may experience rapid eye movements during REM sleep-like states.

20. Body Swaying: Gentle swaying or rocking motions may occur as the subject's body aligns with the hypnotic suggestions.

21. Time Distortion: The subject may perceive time differently, with a few minutes feeling like an extended period.

22. Decreased Blinking: Reduced blinking frequency during relaxation.

23. Fluctuating Breathing Patterns: The breath may alternate between deep and shallow as the trance deepens.

24. Temperature Changes: The subject may feel warmer or cooler as their body regulates in response to the hypnotic experience.

25. Enhanced Sensory Perception: Heightened awareness of sensations like touch, sound, and smell.

26. Changes in Skin Temperature: The skin may feel warmer or cooler to the touch.

27. Reduced Swallowing Reflex: A decrease in the frequency of swallowing during hypnosis.

28. Nystagmus: Involuntary eye movement, often accompanied by increased suggestibility.

29. Time Distortion: The subject may perceive time differently, with a few minutes feeling like an extended period.

30. Cataleptic State: The subject's limbs may become rigid and fixed in a certain position when suggested by the hypnotist.

It's important to remember that not all subjects may exhibit every sign, and individual responses to hypnosis can vary. As a skilled hypnotist, observing these physical indicators will assist you in gauging the depth of trance and tailoring your suggestions to achieve optimal results for each subject.

Verbal Trance Indicators

1. Slow and Monotone Speech: The subject's speech may become slower and more monotonous as they enter a deeper hypnotic state.

2. Softening of Voice: The voice may soften and become more soothing, reflecting a state of relaxation.

3. Repetition: Repeated phrases or words used by the subject, indicating a focused and suggestible state.

4. Yes Set: The subject readily agrees or complies with suggestions, affirming their responsiveness to hypnosis.

5. Imagery and Vivid Descriptions: The subject may use vivid and detailed imagery in their responses or descriptions.

6. Time Distortion: The subject may perceive time differently, expressing that minutes feel like hours or vice versa.

7. Self-Reference: An increase in self-referential language, such as "I feel" or "I see."

8. Loss of Critical Thinking: Decreased skepticism and increased acceptance of suggestions without questioning.

9. Focused Attention: The subject may be fully engaged and focused on the hypnotist's voice and suggestions.

10. Sensory Description: Describing sensations or experiences using all senses, even if not physically present.

11. Emotion Expression: The subject may express heightened emotions, ranging from deep relaxation to joy or calmness.

12. Altered Perception: Describing an altered sense of reality, such as feeling weightless or floating.

13. Confusion or Disorientation: The subject may describe feelings of confusion or disorientation as they dissociate from the external environment.

14. Loss of Awareness: The subject may state a temporary loss of awareness of their surroundings.

15. Absorption in Thoughts: The subject may mention being absorbed in their thoughts or mental imagery.

16. Experiential Language: Using words like "experience," "journey," or "flow" to describe their trance state.

17. Tunnel Vision: Describing a narrowed focus of attention, as if looking through a tunnel.

18. Loss of Sense of Time: The subject may express difficulty in tracking time or feeling like time has passed quickly.

19. Emotional Release: The subject may share experiences of emotional release or catharsis during hypnosis.

20. Heightened Suggestibility: Expressing an increased willingness to accept and act upon hypnotic suggestions.

21. Dissociation: Describing a sense of detachment from their physical body or feeling like an observer.

22. Automatic Responding: The subject may respond automatically to the hypnotist's suggestions without conscious effort.

23. Internal Dialogue: Mentioning an internal dialogue or self-talk during hypnosis.

24. Positive Imagery: The subject may describe positive mental images or scenarios with great enthusiasm.

25. Relaxation and Comfort: Expressing feelings of deep relaxation and comfort during the hypnotic experience.

26. Symbolism: Using symbolic language to describe their thoughts or emotions during trance.

27. Altered Perception of Pain: Describing a reduced perception of pain or discomfort.

28. Self-Discovery: Expressing insights or revelations about themselves during hypnosis.

29. Surrendering Control: The subject may mention surrendering control to the hypnotist's guidance.

30. Increased Self-Awareness: Expressing a heightened sense of self-awareness or self-reflection.

Remember that verbal trance indicators may vary from person to person, and not all subjects will exhibit every sign. As a skilled hypnotist, actively listening to and identifying these verbal cues will allow you to gauge the depth of trance and tailor your suggestions to achieve the desired outcomes for each individual. The effective use of verbal trance indicators, combined with non-verbal cues and deepening techniques, will contribute to successful and impactful hypnosis sessions.

Understanding Abreactions in Hypnosis

In the captivating world of hypnosis, the journey into the subconscious can lead to powerful emotional releases known as abreactions. As a skilled hypnotist, developing a profound understanding of these transformative moments is essential to ensure a safe and rewarding experience for your subjects. Abreactions are emotional outbursts or cathartic releases that occur during hypnosis, unveiling deep-seated feelings and memories that have been buried within the subconscious mind. Embracing these moments with empathy and compassion can lead to profound breakthroughs and lasting positive changes for your subjects.

Abreactions can take various forms, including intense emotional expressions such as crying, laughing, or expressing fear. It is vital to distinguish between an abreaction and a negative reaction to ensure that the emotional release is therapeutic and healing. These emotional releases are not to be feared or avoided but instead signify that your subject has entered a deep trance state, creating an opportunity for profound transformation.

As a skilled hypnotist, you can identify abreactions by being attuned to physical and verbal cues exhibited by your subjects. Look for signs such as rapid breathing, tears, tense body language, or sudden emotional shifts. Creating a safe and trusting environment is paramount to encourage subjects to explore their emotions freely without restraint.

Understanding the causes and triggers of abreactions can provide valuable insights into your subject's psyche. Past traumas, unresolved emotions, and subconscious resistance to suggestions are common factors that can trigger an abreaction. As a hypnotist, your sensitivity and awareness will help navigate these emotional terrains with finesse and compassion.

When an abreaction occurs, avoid interrupting or suppressing the emotional release. Instead, provide unwavering support, allowing the process to unfold naturally. Reframe these moments as opportunities for growth and healing, embracing the potential for profound change.

One of the most significant benefits of abreactions is the heightened suggestibility of the subject's subconscious mind during these moments. Utilize this unique state to reinforce positive affirmations, instill empowering beliefs, and promote lasting change in your subject's life.

After the hypnosis session, offer post-abreaction support to your subjects, giving them space to process their experiences. Provide guidance on integrating the insights gained during hypnosis into their daily lives, nurturing the seeds of transformation that were sown during the session.

Preventive measures are essential to prepare your subjects for the possibility of an abreaction. Educate them about the healing potential of emotional releases, fostering a sense of trust and openness.

Working with subjects experiencing abreactions can be a profoundly rewarding experience for both you and your subjects. Embrace these moments as opportunities to facilitate profound transformations and empower your subjects to overcome emotional barriers. Each abreaction is a unique step towards unlocking the unlimited potential of the human mind and embarking on a transformative journey of self-discovery.

The Power of Hypnotic Language: The Power Words

In world of hypnosis, language holds the key to unlocking the hidden potential of the subconscious mind. Words possess an enchanting ability to bridge the gap between conscious awareness and the deeper realms of the mind. Among the many linguistic treasures at your disposal, power words stand out as a potent force in guiding subjects into hypnotic trances and delivering compelling suggestions.

Power words serve as powerful linkages, subtly weaving suggestions into the fabric of the subject's consciousness. These words act as gateways, inviting the subconscious mind to embrace new beliefs and perspectives willingly. By skillfully employing power words, you can tap into the immense reservoirs of the imagination and shape transformative experiences for your subjects.

Understanding the magic of power words begins with recognizing their influence on the psyche. Simple yet impactful, power words hold the potential to evoke emotions, spark vivid imagery, and facilitate a heightened state of suggestibility. Among these wondrous linguistic tools, four stand out as particularly influential: "If," "It means," "Whenever," "And," and "Because."

1. "If": A Gateway to Possibility

"If" introduces a realm of potential and possibility to the subconscious mind. It encourages subjects to explore new perspectives and outcomes, opening the door to transformative change. For instance, "If you allow yourself to relax completely, you will experience a profound sense of peace."

2. "It means": Assigning New Meanings

"It means" invites the subconscious to attach fresh meanings to familiar experiences. By framing situations differently, you can lead your subjects towards positive interpretations. For example, "When you see the color blue, it means you are tapping into a deep sense of tranquility and inner calm."

3. "Whenever": Embedding Suggestions in Time

"Whenever" instills suggestions as reliable triggers for specific actions. It anchors positive behaviors to specific cues, encouraging your subjects to respond automatically. "Whenever you hear the word 'confidence,' you will feel an unwavering belief in your abilities."

4. "And": Connecting Ideas Harmoniously

"And" acts as a seamless connector, linking suggestions together to create a harmonious flow of thoughts. It encourages the subconscious mind to accept new concepts as part of a unified whole. For instance,

"Relax your body, and let go of any tension. Feel a sense of serenity spreading throughout your being."

5. "Because": Justifying the Power of Suggestion

"Because" presents compelling reasons for accepting suggestions, anchoring them in logical foundations. By providing a rationale, you enhance the subject's willingness to embrace the suggestion. "Close your eyes and take deep breaths, because relaxation is the first step towards achieving your goals."

Harnessing the full potential of power words involves weaving them into your suggestions with intention and finesse. Craft your language with precision, painting vivid images that resonate with your subject's desires and aspirations. Empower your words with emotion, infusing them with sincerity and authenticity to establish a deep connection with your subjects.

Here is a comprehensive list of power words to infuse your language with persuasive impact:

- Transform
- Discover
- Imagine
- Intuitively
- Effortlessly
- Uncover
- Experience

- Harmoniously
- Embrace
- Awaken
- Embody
- Integrate
- Radiate
- Gratitude
- Illuminate
- Empower
- Align
- Connect
- Instinctively

Mastering the art of power words allows you to paint compelling narratives that guide your subjects on a journey of self-discovery and transformation. As you refine your linguistic palette, you will witness the profound influence of words in unlocking the hidden potentials of the human mind and facilitating remarkable hypnotic experiences.

Building Instant Rapport

Building a strong rapport with your subjects is the cornerstone of successful hypnosis. Establishing a deep connection allows you to gain their trust and create a receptive environment for hypnotic suggestions. In this chapter, we will explore some powerful techniques for building instant rapport:

1. Mirroring: Mirroring is a powerful technique that involves subtly imitating your subject's body language, gestures, and postures. By matching their movements, you create a sense of familiarity and unity, signaling to the subconscious mind that you are on the same wavelength. For example, if your subject leans forward or crosses their arms, you can mirror these actions in a natural and non-obvious manner.

2. Cross-Mirroring: Similar to mirroring, cross-mirroring involves matching your subject's body language, but in a more subtle and inconspicuous manner. This technique can be particularly useful in situations where overt mirroring might be too obvious. For instance, if your subject leans back, you might adjust your position slightly to reflect their posture.

3. Echoing: Echoing is a technique that involves repeating key words or phrases used by your subject. By reflecting their language back to them, you demonstrate that you are attentive and understanding, reinforcing the bond between you. For example, if your subject says, "I feel relaxed," you can respond with,

"That's great to hear. Feeling relaxed is essential for this process."

4. Eye Contact: Maintaining appropriate eye contact during the session is vital for building trust and connection. Engaging eyes communicate sincerity and interest, helping your subject feel at ease and receptive to your guidance. While it's essential to maintain eye contact, remember to balance it with natural breaks to avoid making your subject feel uncomfortable.

5. Tonality of Voice: The tone of your voice can have a powerful impact on the hypnotic experience. A calm, soothing, and reassuring tone exudes confidence and warmth, making your subject feel safe and comfortable during the process. For example, using a gentle and steady tone while guiding them into relaxation can help induce a deeper trance.

6. Pacing of Voice: Adjusting the pace of your voice is crucial for maintaining engagement and attentiveness. A moderate and rhythmic pace can induce relaxation, while a faster pace can create excitement and anticipation. For example, during the induction phase, you might use a slower pace to encourage relaxation and later increase the pace to evoke enthusiasm and motivation.

Examples of Rapport-Building Scenarios:

Scenario 1: Mirroring

Subject: *crosses arms*

Hypnotist: *subtly crosses arms in a natural manner*

Subject: *leans forward*

Hypnotist: *leans forward slightly*

Scenario 2: Echoing

Subject: "I've been feeling stressed lately."

Hypnotist: "Feeling stressed lately, huh? It's entirely normal to experience stress."

Scenario 3: Eye Contact

Hypnotist: *maintains steady eye contact while speaking calmly*

Subject: *feels reassured and connected, deepening the rapport*

By combining these rapport-building techniques, you create a harmonious and trusting relationship with your subjects. The more genuinely you can connect with them, the more open and receptive they become to the transformative power of hypnosis. Always remember to be attentive, empathetic, and flexible in your approach, as each person responds uniquely to rapport-building methods. With consistent practice and dedication, you will master the art of building instant rapport and elevate your hypnotic skills to new heights.

Mastering Compliance for Effective Inductions

In this pivotal chapter, we will delve deep into the art of mastering compliance for successful hypnotic inductions. Compliance is the cornerstone of hypnotic influence, and as you harness the power of compliance techniques, you will find yourself seamlessly guiding subjects into profound states of trance.

1. The Yes Set Technique:

The Yes Set is a versatile and fundamental compliance technique used in various forms of communication. By framing a series of statements or questions that evoke positive responses, you pave the way for subjects to enter a receptive mindset. Keep in mind that the subconscious mind is wired to seek agreement, making the Yes Set an excellent tool to foster cooperation.

Example 1: A Sales Pitch

Salesperson: "You value high-quality products, don't you?" (Subject responds "yes.")

Salesperson: "You appreciate exceptional customer service, right?" (Subject responds "yes.")

Salesperson: "And, of course, you desire the best value for your money?" (Subject responds "yes.")

Example 2: A Political Rally

Politician: "We all want a brighter future for our children, don't we?" (Audience responds with agreement.)

Politician: "Education is vital for the progress of our society, isn't it?" (Audience agrees.)

Politician: "A strong economy benefits us all, doesn't it?" (Audience responds affirmatively.)

Example 3: A Motivational Seminar

Speaker: "You believe in the power of positive thinking, don't you?" (Audience responds "yes.")

Speaker: "You know that every challenge is an opportunity for growth, right?" (Audience agrees.)

Speaker: "And you understand that you have the potential to achieve greatness within you?" (Audience responds "yes.")

2. The Agreement Pattern:

The Agreement Pattern relies on presenting undeniable or universally accepted statements that elicit agreement from subjects. By emphasizing shared beliefs and values, you establish rapport and create an environment conducive to the hypnotic process.

Example 1: A Pastor's Sermon

Pastor: "We can all agree that kindness and compassion are essential virtues, can't we?" (Congregation agrees.)

Pastor: "We understand the importance of forgiveness in our lives, don't we?" (Congregation responds "yes.")

Pastor: "And we know that love and understanding can heal even the deepest wounds, right?" (Congregation agrees.)

Example 2: A Marketing Campaign

Company: "We can all appreciate the convenience of our new product, can't we?" (Target audience agrees.)

Company: "We understand that quality is of utmost importance to you, right?" (Target audience responds "yes.")

Company: "And because we value your satisfaction, we have tailored this product to meet your specific needs." (Target audience agrees.)

Example 3: A Life Coach's Workshop

Coach: "We all believe that growth and self-improvement are lifelong journeys, don't we?" (Participants respond "yes.")

Coach: "We recognize that setbacks are opportunities for learning and growth, right?" (Participants agree.)

Coach: "And we understand that setting clear goals is the first step toward achieving success in any endeavor." (Participants respond "yes.")

3. The Foot on the Door Technique (Small Compliance Set):

The Foot on the Door technique is a powerful method of gaining compliance by starting with a small request that is easy for subjects to agree to. Once subjects have taken this initial step, they become more likely to comply with larger requests that follow.

Example 1: A Fundraiser Event

Fundraiser: "Would you be willing to sign our petition for a cause you care about?" (Subject agrees.)

Fundraiser: "Fantastic! Now that you've signed the petition, would you also consider making a small donation to support our cause?" (Subject is more likely to comply after the initial agreement.)

Example 2: A Volunteer Recruitment Drive

Organizer: "Could you spare a few hours to help us with a community project?" (Volunteer agrees.)

Organizer: "Wonderful! Since you're already volunteering, would you mind helping us spread the word and invite more people to join?" (Volunteer is more likely to comply after the initial agreement.)

Example 3: A Subscription Service

Company: "Would you like to receive our free trial for a month?" (Customer agrees.)

Company: "Great! Now that you've experienced our service, would you consider subscribing for a year for a discounted rate?" (Customer is more likely to comply after the initial agreement.)

By mastering compliance and understanding the intricacies of hypnotic language and techniques, you will elevate your hypnotic abilities and create transformative experiences for your subjects. Whether you are using hypnosis for therapeutic purposes or personal development, your newfound expertise in compliance will propel you toward becoming a skilled hypnotist, capable of guiding others toward positive change and self-discovery.

Exploring Hypnosis Careers and Embracing the Art To Help Other People

In this chapter, we will explore the diverse and fulfilling career opportunities available for skilled hypnotists. Hypnosis, with its remarkable ability to facilitate positive changes in individuals, is a powerful tool that opens doors to a variety of professional paths.

1. Clinical Hypnotherapy:

Clinical hypnotherapy offers a rewarding career, helping clients achieve profound transformation and personal growth. Working in collaboration with medical professionals, you may assist in pain management, habit control, and addressing underlying emotional issues. Your expertise as a hypnotist can complement traditional medical treatments, providing holistic care to those in need.

2. Consulting Hypnotist:

As a consulting hypnotist, you have the freedom to establish your practice and work with a wide range of clients. Whether you choose to specialize in weight management, smoking cessation, stress reduction, political consulting, or business and marketing strategies, your skills can make a significant difference in people's lives. Consulting hypnotists often build lasting relationships with their clients, fostering trust and a supportive environment for personal growth.

3. Stage Hypnosis and Entertainment:

For those with a flair for the dramatic, stage hypnosis offers an exciting avenue. Captivating audiences with mesmerizing displays of hypnotic phenomena, you can entertain and inspire through unforgettable performances. Stage hypnotists are known for their charisma and showmanship, and their ability to create an atmosphere of wonder and amusement.

4. Hypnosis Workshops and Training:

Beyond individual sessions, conducting workshops and training programs can be immensely rewarding. Sharing your knowledge and expertise in hypnosis with others, you can empower them to improve their lives and help others as well. Workshops may focus on various areas, including stress reduction, confidence building, personal growth, political consulting strategies, or even business and marketing techniques, and can attract diverse audiences seeking positive change.

5. Hypnosis as a Keynote Speaker:

As a certified hypnotist, you possess unique insights into the human mind and behavior. These insights can make you a compelling keynote speaker, capable of captivating audiences and inspiring them to tap into their full potential. Your ability to communicate the power of the subconscious mind can leave a lasting impact on listeners and drive them toward personal transformation.

6. Motivational Speaker and Trainer:

Hypnotists often possess exceptional communication skills and a deep understanding of human behavior. These qualities make them highly effective motivational speakers and trainers. As a motivational speaker, you can inspire and uplift audiences, igniting a spark of motivation and instilling a sense of purpose in their lives.

7. Sales Trainer and Influencer:

Hypnosis is the art of influencing the mind, and this skillset can be invaluable in the realm of sales and marketing. As a hypnotist, you can use your expertise to train sales teams in persuasive techniques, effective communication, building rapport with clients, and leveraging powerful hypnotic language patterns to enhance marketing strategies.

8. Political Consultant:

In the realm of politics, the ability to influence and persuade is paramount. As a skilled hypnotist, you can leverage your expertise in hypnosis to become a political consultant. By assisting political candidates in enhancing their communication skills, public speaking, and charisma, you can contribute significantly to their success on the campaign trail.

Embracing the Power of Hypnosis:

Hypnosis is a gateway to self-discovery, personal growth, and success. It serves as a bridge to the subconscious mind, unlocking its hidden reservoirs of potential and fostering profound change from within. Hypnosis empowers individuals to overcome obstacles, harness their strengths, and manifest their dreams into reality.

As a passionate advocate of hypnosis and its life-changing benefits, I offer workshops on hypnosis and Neuro-Linguistic Programming (NLP) on my website, **www.coachbillyg.com**. These programs provide comprehensive training for individuals eager to explore the transformative world of hypnosis and NLP, including applications in business, marketing, political consulting, and more. Additionally, I am available for keynote speaking engagements, sharing my expertise and experiences to inspire and motivate audiences from all walks of life.

Hypnosis is a remarkable tool that can guide you toward a more fulfilling and purposeful life. Whether you aspire to become a professional hypnotist, delve into political consulting, or simply want to explore the depths of your mind, hypnosis offers infinite possibilities and a journey of self-discovery.

SUMMARY

Congratulations on completing your journey in learning hypnosis! You have taken a remarkable step towards unlocking the untapped potential of your mind and unleashing the power of hypnosis. It is truly inspiring to witness your dedication to personal growth and the pursuit of knowledge.

Throughout this book, we have demystified the world of hypnosis, delved into its fascinating techniques, and explored its transformative effects. Together, we have ventured into the depths of the subconscious mind, harnessing the power of suggestion, and understanding the art of deepening the hypnotic state.

With different types of induction methods, deepeners, and suggestions at your fingertips, you are now equipped to guide others and yourself into profound states of relaxation, focus, and positive change. By mastering the power of rapport building and compliance techniques, you can establish trust and create lasting impressions with your subjects.

But remember, with great power comes great responsibility. As you venture forth on your journey as a hypnotist, always prioritize ethics and integrity. Your intentions must be pure, and your goal should be to empower and uplift those you influence.

This book is only the beginning of your exploration into the world of hypnosis. The possibilities are endless as you embark on a path of helping others tap into their subconscious potential and bring about positive transformations.

To further your knowledge, I encourage you to visit my website, **www.coachbillyg.com**, where you can find workshops, resources, and opportunities to enhance your skills as a hypnotist. Connect with me through social media to stay informed about the latest developments in the field.

Before we part ways, I want to leave you with this thought: You have the power to make a profound impact on yourself and the world around you. Embrace this newfound skill with humility, compassion, and a genuine desire to bring about positive change.

Thank you for joining me on this enlightening journey. Your passion for growth and your dedication to becoming a skilled hypnotist are a testament to your unwavering spirit. I am excited to witness the wonderful transformations you will facilitate through the art of hypnosis.

Wishing you boundless success and a future filled with endless possibilities.

With warmest regards,Coach Billy G.

www.coachbillyg.com

About the Author

Bill Gonzales

Bill Gonzales, a consulting hypnotist and a Neuro-Linguistic Programming (NLP) coach has been continuously practicing the art in coaching, business, and therapies. With a journey into hypnosis that started in 2017, Bill has dedicated himself to demystifying and teaching this transformative art. His workshops and coaching sessions have touched many lives, guiding them towards personal growth.

He is also an entrepreneur and focuses on his Network Business to help and inspire more people to become successful.

Bill's approach is all about making hypnosis accessible. His workshops are engaging and his keynotes inspiring. With his new book, 'Hypnosis 101, he takes readers on a journey into the world of hypnosis, breaking down complex techniques into easy to understand steps. Through his work, Bill is on a mission to help people tap into their potential and lead more fulfilling lives.

www.ingramcontent.com/pod-product-compliance
Lightning Source LLC
LaVergne TN
LVHW041631070526
838199LV00052B/3313